50 POST-MEDIEVAL
AND MODERN FINDS

From the Portable Antiquities Scheme

Laura Burnett & Rob Webley

AMBERLEY

To Beni and Stefan, who put up with a lot of 'quali-finds' talk.

First published 2024

Amberley Publishing
The Hill, Stroud
Gloucestershire, GL5 4EP

www.amberley-books.com

ISBN 978 1 3981 1467 8 (print)
ISBN 978 1 3981 1468 5 (ebook)

British Library Cataloguing in Publication Data.
A catalogue record for this book is available from
the British Library.

Typeset in 10pt on 13pt Celeste.
Typesetting by SJmagic DESIGN SERVICES, India.
Printed in the UK.

Contents

Acknowledgements

The first thank you must go to all the people who have found the objects in this book and reported them to the Portable Antiquities Scheme (PAS) to ensure knowledge about them is not lost and can be shared with everyone.

While we have recorded some of the finds, most were originally recorded by colleagues: other Finds Liaison Officers, assistants, interns and many dedicated volunteers, including self-recorders. Finds Liaison Officers have to be jacks of all trades and for unusual finds rely on freely given help by specialists in certain periods or types of material.

Our thanks go to the following recorders, identifiers and experts on whose work and advice we build: Kurt Adams, Andrew Agate, Jo Ahmet, Steven Ashley, Natasha Awais-Dean, Frank Basford, Angie Bolton, Nonn Bound, Tom Brindle, Margaret Broomfield, Andrew Brown, Anni Byard, Paul Cannon, Julie Cassidy, Alan Charman, Sarahjayne Clements, Robert Collins, Nina Corey, Erica Darch, Adam Daubney, Wenke Domscheit, Beth Echtenacher, Martin Foreman, Hazel Forsyth, Megan Gard, Helen Geake, Teresa Gilmore, Rebecca Griffiths, Jane Hanbidge, Ciorstaidh Hayward Trevarthen, Richard Henry, David Higgins, Phil Hughes, Andrzej Janowski, Rachel King, Rebecca Lang, Mark Lodwick, Chris Lovell, Frances McIntosh, Laura McLean, Katie Marsden, Simon Maslin, Alan Massey, Samantha Matthews, Marc Meltonville, Des Murphy, John Naylor, Simon Nicholson, Stuart Noon, Vanessa Oakden, Tim Pestell, Carolina Rangel de Lima, Peter Reavill, Nina Steele, Kate Sumnall, Dora Thornton, Anna Tyacke, Ros Tyrrell, Rachel Tyson, Bruce Wales, Julian Watters, Benjamin Westwood, Alex Whitlock, David Williams, Hugh Wilmott, Arwen Wood, Danielle Wootton, Paul Wragg, and Stuart Wyatt. Particular mention must be made of the late Geoff Egan, who not only provided advice on a number of the finds in this book but was a big inspiration behind our work on this subject.

Jonathan Burnett, Nick Collins, Rhiannon Davies, Emily Hogg, Naomi Payne and Hannah Webley were kind enough to read through and advise on the text – their comments and suggestions have made it more accurate and interesting. We are also very grateful to Annemarieke Willemsen for agreeing to write the book's foreword.

All images, unless indicated in the text, are copyright of the Portable Antiquities Scheme and the local hosts of its Finds Liaison Officers. Thanks are due to all providers for allowing these pictures to be reused in this book and to the other photographers and museums who have made their images available free of copyright. Every attempt has been made to seek permissions and attribute images correctly; however, we apologise for any errors and will make the necessary corrections at the earliest opportunity.

Tin-glazed tile in the Dutch style showing an elephant, one of Annemarieke Willemsen's favourite PAS finds. Probably made in London between 1590 and 1620 and found on the Thames foreshore, 92 mm long (LON-14BFBD).

Foreword

I love the post-medieval period, and I love small finds. Both have the power to build bridges between the past and our own lives, as they are the objects of daily life, from centuries we can imagine well.

Even though most archaeologists are inclined to the very distant past, from prehistory and Roman times to the Middle Ages, it's finds from the sixteenth to twentieth centuries that can always count on the public's fascination. Artefacts from excavations from the post-medieval and modern era can often be recognised easily. Spoons, toy soldiers, buttons, dog collars, old coins... They combine recognition of the time that passed with a sort of nostalgia: these people dressed differently, but they were the same as us.

Our understanding of the daily lives of people in the past has greatly increased by the data from the wonderful Portable Antiquities Scheme. Many categories of inconspicuous metal objects, like dress accessories and badges, were never interesting enough to keep, or to be depicted or written about. But they have now come to light in great quantities to reveal a far more detailed and decorated image of the lives of our ancestors.

I am thankful to the compilers of this book, both authorities on small metal finds from the not-too-distant past and protagonists of the Portable Antiquities Scheme. They prove that small finds can be great ambassadors for the added value of archaeology to history, and allow us to come close to the twenty generations of common people that preceded the twenty-first century.

Dr Annemarieke Willemsen
Curator of Medieval and Later Collections
National Museum of Antiquities, Leiden

Introduction

This book does not tell the last 500 years of English and Welsh history through objects. We have not started with the period's big events and changes and looked for objects that illustrate them. Instead we started with the objects recorded by the Portable Antiquities Scheme (PAS) and have tried to tell their stories. There are, of course, many objects whose stories are entwined with the big events: huge rises in population; rising health and living standards; civil and world wars; the change in a political system from monarchy to widening democracy; growing literacy and availability of information; and industrialisation and globalisation. Many other objects tell private, local, or small stories: a child's shoe, a successful female entrepreneur, or a night of dancing.

Compared to a book about Bronze Age or Roman finds it may seem odd to focus on understanding this period through objects. It is the time from which we have the most written records, pictures, and, later, photos and videos. Archaeology's contribution might therefore be less obvious, but it has great potential to connect us to people's lived experience. Artefacts provide important evidence where records may not exist, such as of people's private beliefs, social lives and informal dress. They bear witness to those less likely to appear in historical records, such as the poor and children. Objects also provide a tangible link to events. In doing so they confront us with the reality and the experience of the individual humans who lived through this most formative of periods. This book is thronged with things – beautiful, intriguing things – but we hope it will also feel thronged with people: from Henry VIII and Katherine of Aragon to a seventeenth-century distiller, and from German prisoners of war to children playing with treasured toys.

All the objects in this book were found across England and Wales and recorded by the Portable Antiquities Scheme. The Scheme records objects found by the public, rather than from excavations. Some finds qualify as Treasure and legally have to be reported. The vast majority, however, do not and have been voluntarily offered for recording by members of the public, including metal detectorists, gardeners, builders and mudlarks. They have shared their finds with the Scheme so they can be available to everyone to learn from and enjoy. You can find more detail about the Scheme at the end of this book; you can also find out how to record your finds and about the legal process of Treasure at finds.org.uk. More details about all the finds in this book can be found on the website's database; the database number is given for each object (e.g. WMID-A51F34 or SUSS-05BC17).

One of the joys of objects is that they simultaneously reflect their individual creators, their users, and the times they live in more broadly. This also made it tricky to decide which of our themed chapters to put each find in. For example, this small model of an aeroplane may have been a toy, or a fashionable brooch. It is made from a reused, worn or smoothed coin, cut and folded using simple tools. Such models were often made by aircraft ground crew in the Second World War to send home to loved ones and are known as 'Penny spitfires'. It could have gone in almost any of our chapters.

Choosing the title of this book was a topic of long debate. The 'Roman' or 'medieval' periods have wide recognition, for both specialists and the public, but the bit that comes after the medieval – though recognisably different from our industrial, modern world – is less clearly named. At school you probably studied the Tudor, Stuart, Georgian or Victorian periods, or labelled things by century: eighteenth-, nineteenth-, or twentieth-century history. A list of dynasties, or centuries, would have led to a very long title, and naming these periods after royal dynasties has also fallen out of favour amongst professionals. Calling the period after the monarchs may suggest that is where we should focus our study, but most parts of ordinary people's lives, and the objects they use, were not immediately impacted by the change in kings, queens, or even dynasties.

Model plane made from a coin. Found near White Waltham airfield, Berkshire, 32 mm long (SUR-97E596).

This book is called *50 Post-Medieval and Modern Finds* because that is how these finds are referred to on the PAS database and by archaeologists. The early sixteenth century had a lot in common with the medieval period before it and some of our earliest finds reflect this. From the mid-sixteenth century, radical change in the way people lived and worked, and speedier and more frequent connections to Africa and Asia, plus new connections to the Americas, meant people of the time were very conscious of living in a changing world. Historians often call the sixteenth to early eighteenth centuries the 'Early Modern' period to reflect how many of the changes we think of as 'modern', from industrialisation to globalisation, started then, albeit in a smaller way. The seventeenth to nineteenth centuries are often called the 'Age of Revolutions', marking the huge changes in this period. These are not just political revolutions like the French Revolution or the British 'Glorious' Revolution of 1688, they are social and economic revolutions: religious change, the Industrial Revolution, the Agricultural Revolution, the Consumer Revolution, to which we can add the Social and Digital Revolutions of the twentieth and twenty-first centuries.

Picking just fifty finds from the nearly quarter of a million objects from this period recorded by the PAS was a major challenge. We have included a lot of images of supplementary objects, which hopefully help enhance the story of each main find. We have tried to reflect common finds from the period, as well as the unusual – homemade objects as well as expensive gold jewellery. The map and timeline on the next pages can help you find artefacts of specific dates or from particular areas. The earliest finds are from 1500, and the latest from 2008, but they do cluster in the first two centuries, reflecting the Scheme's prioritising of pre-1700 objects. The objects are arranged thematically, but each is a self-contained piece and the book can be read in any order. These are our, perhaps idiosyncratic, choices and we hope that you will enjoy discovering more about them and the people who once used and treasured them.

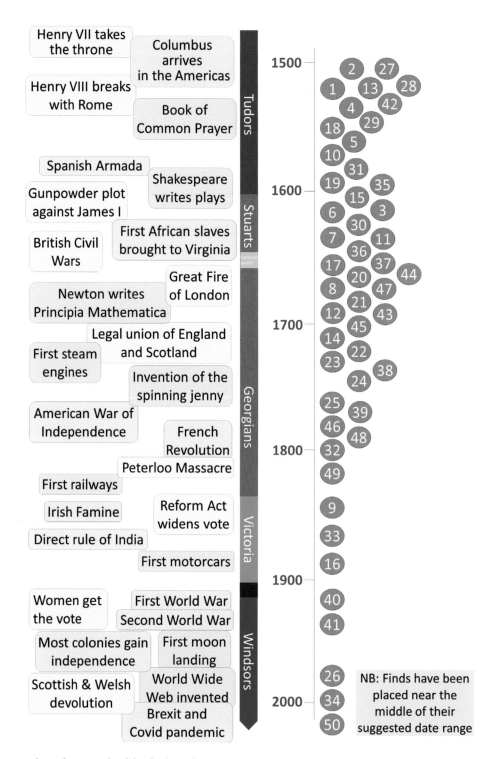

Timeline showing the fifty finds and important events. Pre-1700 finds are prioritised for recording by PAS so are more common on the database.

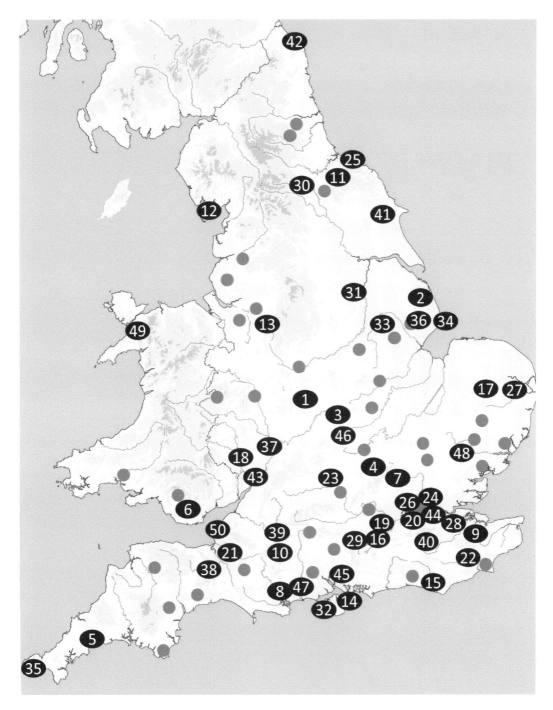

Map of all the finds. The main fifty finds are numbered; the green dots represent other finds pictured in the book.

Fashion

We often think of fashion as something very short term, perhaps having less impact than technological changes, but because of its flexibility, fashion often allows us to see people's individual and social choices more clearly. In these objects we have tried to explore not just beautiful and fascinating pieces, but also some of the underlying behaviours, beliefs and feelings that influenced these choices. As well as reflecting people's decisions and beliefs, objects also actively shape them. A belt hook such as Find 2 or a seal matrix like Find 9 reflects a level of wealth and a certain position, and also reinforces that position in the mind of the owner and others, whenever it is viewed and used.

Hand-spun and hand-woven cloth, or even early machine-made cloth, was expensive. Well into the twentieth century clothing was often one of the most expensive things people owned. Clothing was repaired and reused by others until it became rags, which could be used in turn, eventually ending up in the fields as a way to improve soils. The cloth, and buttons and lace tags such as Find 4, could be reused into new garments or sold on. Clothing was also a store of wealth; jewellery such as Find 1 was appreciated for its design but also for its financial value.

Fashion plate from an early edition of the world's first fashion magazine, published in Paris in 1787. (Courtesy of the Rijksmuseum, Amsterdam)

1. Necklace (WMID-A51F34)
1509–33
Found in Warwickshire, in 2019. Weight 317 g.

This stunning necklace comprises a gold heart-shaped pendant found with its chain formed of seventy-five interlocking links of gold. The pendant was suspended from a gripping hand emanating from a golden cloud. Detailing on the hand is remarkable – even the fingernails are shown. On the cuff, speckling in black on a white enamel ground suggests an ermine trim to a red sleeve. The weight of the necklace, made in 98 per cent pure gold, as well as the extensive enamel work, implies a high-status owner. A few details do suggest it was made hurriedly, though, perhaps as part of a group.

The pendant's decoration hints at the most elevated of social associations. On one side the field is filled with a pair of entwined branches, engraved to take enamel, and culminating in a Tudor rose and pomegranate. These represent the union of Henry VIII and Katherine of Aragon; the other side features their initials 'h' and 'K', connected by an interlaced ribbon. Both sides have the same inscription: 'TOVS IORS' in Lombardic script on an unfurled banner. Meaning 'always' in French, this may also be a pun if the second word is read in English – 'all yours'.

This stunning object must date from the period of Henry and Katherine's marriage (1509–33). Multiple similar pieces may have been made for members of the court, or as gifts in association with royal events, such as foreign embassies or jousts in the 1510s or 1520s. While royal marriages were important diplomatically, this object shows how important it was, for Henry and Katherine, but also others, to portray them as entwined in a romantic partnership.

The back of the pendant; it was
x-rayed, and opened, but was
empty.

Gold necklace with enamel decoration (WMID-A51F34).

This gilded silver badge combines a rose with a pomegranate and was a more affordable commemoration of Henry and Katherine's marriage, or of her earlier engagement to Henry's brother, Arthur. Found in South Molton, Devon, 22 mm high (DEV-1C5D34).

14

2. Belt hook (NLM-6B44E4)
1475–1525
Found in Muckton, Lincolnshire, in 2017. Length 57 mm.

A man posing in a fancy outfit, hand on hip, and a dancing couple enliven these practical objects. They would have been hung on a belt from the long clip on the back. At the base is a tube to hold a large ring of household keys. The keys would be for doors but also chests and cupboards holding valuable goods like spices.

Such belt hooks, or *Gürtelhaken*, are rare finds in England, as they were made, and mostly used, in the areas which make up modern-day Germany. The individual on this example wears a hood and has a notably short tunic, in an 'Italian style'. Other belt hooks show people in fashions characteristic of both the later fifteenth and sixteenth centuries.

Belt fittings like these, for the suspension of keys or other implements, are known as chatelaines. They were practical objects but also a status symbol, indicating the mistress of the house who held the keys. It is no surprise that the majority of them have been found in eastern England. This area has always had links to Central and Northern Europe, through trade, marriages and people moving between the areas for work, in this period often in the cloth trade.

Above left: Belt hook in the shape of a posing man (NLM-6B44E4).

Above right: The only other belt hook of German type recorded by the PAS to date features a dancing couple. Found in Acton, Suffolk, 57 mm long (SF-713A5B).

15

3. 'Visard' mask (NARC-151A67)
1500–1750
Found in Kilsby, Northamptonshire, in 2010. Length 195 mm.

This mask would be worn while travelling or outside, to protect the face. In the post-medieval period having a tan or weather-roughened skin was associated with poverty. Richer women who could afford not to work in the fields were keen to preserve pale, unweathered skin, sometimes even using poisonous, white lead-based make-up.

The mask is made of luxury black velvet, some of which is now faded, and lined with silk. The slit at the base would have been sewn together to make the mask slightly shaped over the face. There are no ties – it was held in place by the bead attached by the mouth, which the wearer held between their teeth. This slightly awkward attachment made it quick and easy to put on and take off as the wearer went in and out of the sun. It would also have made it harder for the wearer to speak, but contemporary discussion suggests their use, in England at least, had more to do with vanity than silencing women. Contemporary male commentators worried that the anonymity they provided gave women freedom to avoid being identified and greeted by men in the street, encouraged women to attend disreputable activities, and could be used for nefarious purposes.

This example was found within a wall of a sixteenth-century house. This could be for concealment by the owner, to keep it safe or to avoid having to wear it, or for similar witchcraft protection as the shoes discussed with Find 33. While we know such masks existed from some sources and drawings, they do not survive in costume collections and are seldom shown in portraits, so this find is really important in understanding more about this practice.

The visard was found folded, so one half of its front is dirtier than the other (NARC-151A67). The small, black glass bead is visible by the mouth.

A fashionably dressed English woman wearing a similar mask, from a book of drawings made by a German soldier in 1595. (Courtesy of the Los Angeles County Museum of Art)

4. Gold and enamelled lace tag (BUC-E33633)
1500–50
Found near Wing, Buckinghamshire, in 2011. Length 20 mm.

As well as buttons, laces were used to fasten clothing and fit it to the body. Laced ties and ribbons were used at the waist and cuffs, where today we might use elastic. Bodices were usually laced, and in certain periods there were fashions for laced sleeves, jackets, and coats. Metal ends on laces and ties made them easier to thread, and people also used special needles called bodkins to lace ribbons through garments. In the sixteenth century lace ends were elaborated into large tags, called aglets, as fashionable decoration on clothes. Pieces like this beautiful gold and enamelled example are shown in portraits of royalty and nobility; men and women wore them in pairs down their sleeves and men also wore them on hats. This example was found squashed from its original cylindrical shape. Only small sections of the white enamel, which would have filled each cell, remain and any other coloured background enamel has been lost.

Above: Lace end (aglet) (BUC-E33633).

Right: Portrait of Francis I of France, painted in the 1530s, showing him wearing aglets on his slashed doublet, the sleeves of his overcoat and even on his hat. (Courtesy of The Met, New York)

Silver bodkins became fashionable in the seventeenth century. As well as a practical way to lace ribbons through garments they were also worn as hair jewellery. This example has a maker's mark stamped on one face and the owner's initials, 'M C', hand engraved on the other. Found in Pulham Market, Norfolk, 142 mm long (NMS-032A66).

5. Silver-gilt dress hook (CORN-2D1372)
1500–1600
Found in Carlyon, Cornwall, in 2018. Length 34 mm.

Many of the objects in this chapter can be recognised from portraits, or were widely discussed by contemporaries. Decorative dress hooks, by contrast, like this example, were not widely known before thousands started being found by metal-detectorists and recorded through the PAS. They all have loops to be sewn to clothing, but there is still debate about how they were worn and it is likely that sharp-hooked ones had different purposes to the blunt-hooked ones like Find 37.

Some with sharp hooks, like this, were possibly used to hold the point of a linen shawl or neckerchief in place at the back. Others may have been used in pairs on a strap around the waist to hook into the wide ends of skirts, hitching them up above the muddy ground when outside. As people's backs – and people walking in muddy streets – are seldom shown in paintings, they are difficult to identify. We do know they were worn by lots of women and come in a range of materials and decoration, to suit all budgets and tastes.

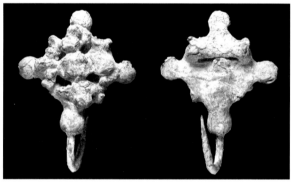

Above left: Silver-gilt dress hook with sewing slot on the back and hook at the base (CORN-2D1372).

Above right: Example in a lead-tin alloy, like pewter, with a sewing loop on the back. This material was cheap and easy to cast into complex shapes but would have been very weak and easily broken in use. Found near Pyecombe, West Sussex, 40 mm long (SUSS-0289F7).

Left: This openwork scene of St George spearing a dragon looks elaborate but could be easily cast in an open-topped mould. Found in Brookland, Kent, 44 mm long (KENT-CC324B).

6. Copper-alloy spur (NMGW-69B4FE)
1600–50
Found in Llantrisant, Rhondda Cynon Taf, in 2013. Length 77 mm.

The wearing of spurs as an item of fashion has developed through time, alongside use as a practical riding aid. While emblematic of knighthood in the Middle Ages, the fashionable importance of spurs is considered to reach its high point in the seventeenth century. By this time, a spur with a separate spiked wheel (rowel) had long been the norm. However, for the first time since the late thirteenth century, in the early to mid-seventeenth century there was a brief revival of the prick spur. Known as 'Scotch' spurs, probably for James I (who was king of Scotland before also inheriting the crown of England and Wales), this type has gently curved sides and a bent neck. The goad has four protruding lobes in a cruciform arrangement before a small point. Further embellishment includes moulded ridges on the sides and neck, while other 'Scotch' spurs featured decoration made of punched annulets.

'Scotch' spur with the goad, neck and part of the curved arms to fit around the heel (NMGW-69B4FE).

This 'Scotch' (prick) spur has detailed stamped decoration. Found in Marston Magna, Somerset, now 51 mm long (SOM-F42C16).

Detail from a 1630s portrait showing fashionable spurs, with rowels rather than a goad, and boots which pulled up over the knee to protect from mud. (Courtesy of the Rijksmuseum, Amsterdam/Europeana)

7. Enamelled button with a lion (BH-DEE512)
1625–75
Found in Redbourn, Hertfordshire, in 2012. Diameter 25 mm.

Buttons, as opposed to ties and toggles, started to be used widely to fasten clothes from the thirteenth century, allowing a closer fit. In the seventeenth and particularly the eighteenth century buttons became larger and more decorative, while still being used for fastening. Some were used in pairs at the neck of a cloak or coat with a link or chain between them. They are found in many different materials, making them accessible to a wider range of society. This example, with its running lion, is part of a group of enamelled objects made in London around the middle of the seventeenth century. The blue and white enamel was added into cast recesses around raised areas of the shiny metal, a new production technique, which meant they were quicker, and cheaper, to produce.

'Stuart enamel' button with a lion (BH-DEE512).

In the eighteenth century very large, flat buttons called 'dandy' buttons became fashionable. They were designed to reflect the light and were decorated with incised or cut lines and patterns. Found in North Luffenham, Rutland, 17 mm in diameter (LEIC-43DADD).

20

STEEL BUTTONS I   Coup de Bouton

In this eighteenth-century cartoon the gentleman's buttons are so large and shiny the reflected light is blinding. (Print originally published 1777 by W. Humphrey. Courtesy of Lewis Walpole Library, Yale University, New Haven)

8. Glass perfume bottle (DOR-23C926)
1650–1700
Found in Wimborne Minster, Dorset, in 2007. Height 59 mm.

This very small glass bottle probably held a scent or beauty lotion. High-quality, clear glass like this requires the use of special fluxes such as plants grown in salt-marshes, or quartz or flint as a base and purifiers like manganese. These additions prevented the usual green-brown or pale blue tint caused by iron impurities. At the start of this period such glass was often imported, especially from Venice. In the later sixteenth and seventeenth century the government encouraged the development of local glass production, and by 1700 even window glass was mass produced and affordable to most people, although in small panes. This vessel is very decorative but it was quite hastily and crudely made; the applied foot is so uneven the vessel cannot stand on it. This suggests the contents were the main point of the purchase and were expensive.

Seventeenth-century perfumes might include floral waters, expensive woods and spices, and animal musks. Wider use of newer distilling equipment meant more scents could be extracted, and concentrated, like modern perfumes. Scent was used for pleasure but also to purify the air. It was widely believed, even into the nineteenth century, that bad smells in themselves could cause disease, as opposed to airborne pathogens or the polluted and fetid objects which might be associated with the smell. As well as wearing perfume, people might carry a perfumed cloth, pomander of scented plants, or a small bottle like this, to sniff as they travelled through dirty streets and areas.

Small glass bottle with glass trails down the sides and blob of blue glass on each side, with a pressed pattern (DOR-23C926).

9. Copper-alloy and glass fob seal (SUSS-2D2CC8)
1800–1900
Found near Thurnham, Kent, in 2020. Length 16 mm.

The legal importance of seals to authenticate a document was gradually replaced by signing your name or writing your mark in this period, but seal matrices – the object used as a stamp to make the seal – remained fashionable. Wearing one suggested you wrote lots of letters and sealed business documents. A hanging fob seal, with elaborate top, became a decorative piece of jewellery worn by men and later also by women. The design did not always identify an individual, although some do have coats of arms, but was chosen to display their interests and taste. By the nineteenth century, especially after the invention of lickable envelopes in the 1830s, they were usually entirely decorative. Cheaper examples in gilded copper with glass 'stones' are very common finds and demonstrate the interests of the growing middle and wealthier working classes.

This example has a thistle and 'DINNA FORGET' engraved on it. The legend may come from the Robert Burns poem 'Dinna forget Me' or the popular ballad 'Dinna Forget' by Mrs Millard and John Imrah published in 1831. Scottish songs, symbols (like the thistle), and tartan were very fashionable in the nineteenth century, a trend encouraged by Queen Victoria's love of Scotland and a romanticised Scottish identity.

Nineteenth-century fob seal (SUSS-2D2CC8).

This elaborate gold example has an amethyst engraved 'Remember me' on the base and, in a secret compartment, a lock of hair under glass. Found in Landford, Wiltshire, 29 mm high (HAMP-609305).

Living and Dying

All the finds in this book are about people's lives but those in this chapter are centred around activities we perhaps think of as universal and unchanging: growing up, falling in love, eating, being injured, and dying. While the passage of time and mortality may not change, the way people went about their everyday lives altered a huge amount in this period. From the food people ate, to the houses they lived in, medicine, and even the ways people measured and considered time, all changed. Rather than arrange the finds in this chapter in the usual chronological order, we have broadly arranged them according to the life cycle, from birth to death.

A seventeenth-century Dutch family sits around a fire. The fire is on an open hearth by the wall with a smoke hood over it, rather than in a recessed fireplace. A bed, with a trundle (pull-out) bed for children underneath, is visible in the background. (*Mother feeding new-born baby with spoon?* by A. van Ostade, courtesy of the Wellcome Collection, London)

10. Silver whistle-teether (WILT-6D1427)
1550–1700
Found in Stockton, Wiltshire, in 2015. Length 74 mm.

This baby toy would have held a piece of red coral in the end opposite the whistle. The wire bands would have made it easier to grip and more interesting for a baby to play with, as does the attached bell.

The first two years of a child's life were intensely dangerous throughout this period. From 1550 to 1900 between a fifth and a sixth of children died in the first few years of life. This was much worse in years of epidemic diseases, and death rates were higher in urban areas and if you were poorer. In rapidly growing London the infant mortality rate got worse rather than better, doubling between the sixteenth and mid-eighteenth century, when nearly two-thirds of all babies died before reaching their second birthday. It was only after 1900 that infant mortality rates started to fall rapidly.

The loss of a child was terrible, for parents and families in all periods, and attempts were made to alleviate what were thought of as the risks. The red cheeks, pain and slight temperature that often come with teething were similar to some common childhood illnesses. Teething was thought to be a cause of death in itself, rather than just occurring in the same period that babies were most vulnerable. Red coral from the Mediterranean has been used as an amulet for children and adults since ancient times. Its smooth, hard texture was perfect for a teething baby to chew on, reducing the symptoms, and perceived risk, of teething. This expensive teether therefore had a practical, enjoyable and protective effect for the baby.

Silver whistle-teether
(WILT-6D1427).

26

This *Girl by a High Chair* (1640) has strings of coral and a very fancy gold whistle-teether with bells and rock crystal. (Courtesy of Mauritshuis, The Hague/Europeana)

11. Lead-alloy hornbook (GLO-9F5C77)
1600–1700
Found in Ingleby Greenhow, North Yorkshire, in 2017. Length 39 mm.

On one side this lead-alloy 'hornbook' bears the alphabet in five lines. The letters J and U are omitted; on other objects I and V are often used in their place. There are otherwise no mistakes such as the missing or reversed letters sometimes seen on these 'books'. On the other side of this object are the upside-down letters 'TS'; they are likely to be a moulded maker's mark. Intriguingly, this hornbook may have come from the same mould as another recorded, from Pontefract, around 70 miles away (SWYOR-B234D7). Such objects were more popular in the North and the Midlands, similar to the distribution of flat leaden dolls (see Find 25).

These lead 'hornbooks' are similar to far larger alphabet tablets where the letters were written on paper or vellum and protected by a thin, horn covering. Debate remains as to the function of these lead examples: were they just smaller, simpler versions? Or does their crudeness and similarity to lead dolls of the time suggest they were toys, 'owned' by a doll who could do their lessons alongside their owner? Either way, these objects may relate to aspirational parents in these areas attempting to improve their children's reading skills, and they demonstrate that learning to read, and trace letters, was a familiar part of many children's lives by this time.

Lead-alloy hornbook (GLO-9F5C77).

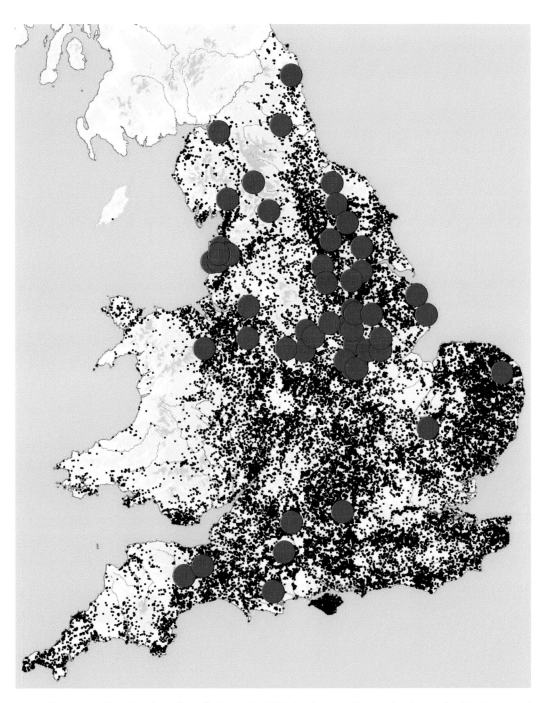

All post-medieval and modern finds on the PAS database, with hornbooks marked by larger red dots. (Map by authors)

12. Silver cufflink element (LANCUM-9F0203)
1660–1700
Found near Stainton with Adgarley, Cumbria, in 2016. Diameter 16 mm.

As well as wedding and engagement rings, often identified by a 'posy' inscription on the inner face, many other objects reflect marriage and relationships. Marriage was often idealised in this period as combining love or strong affection with practical partnership. This silver disc was part of a set of cufflinks, one of a pair connected by a link through the loop on the back. The front is embossed with the design of clasped hands above two small flaming hearts with a crown above. This design is traditionally thought to allude to the marriage of Charles II and Catherine of Braganza in 1662. The popularity of these designs suggests the imagery could be personal, a gift of love or commemoration of a marriage, but it can also be construed as supporting a Catholic or Royalist political stance.

Cufflinks were an entirely new type of object that appeared in the second half of the seventeenth century. They evidence new styles of fashion – of shirt wearing – influenced particularly by the contemporary court of Louis XIV in France. Compared to the previous, often more utilitarian methods of fastening cuffs, cufflink buttons provided small canvases for making discreet political or personal statements.

Above: Disc from a cufflink (LANCUM-9F0203).

Left: The imagery of clasped hands and hearts is also seen on 'fede' (fidelity) rings. This seventeenth-century example has an inscription on the inner face: 'Be true in Hart'. Found in Collingbourne Kingston, Wiltshire, 22 mm in width (WILT-4C20D3).

13. Copper-alloy skillet (NARC-3775C7)
1475–1550
Found in Congleton, Cheshire East, in 2009. Diameter 135 mm.

This skillet is a very rare survival and one of the earliest examples of this type of cooking vessel known in England. It was used over an open fire; there is still soot encrusted on the outside. Cooking vessels like this often broke; broken rims and legs are common finds, but such vessels were one of the more expensive things a poorer person would own, and many are found with repairs. This skillet is unusually complete, with only one leg and most of the handle lost. The remaining legs have worn to different lengths from being dragged back and forth on a stone hearth.

The skillet is similar in size to a modern saucepan and could be used to fry food, make sauces or cook a smaller meal. Inventories of people's possessions show that in the sixteenth and seventeenth centuries people started buying more small 'brass' pots and skillets, like this one, allowing them to cook different parts of the meal separately, and try new recipes and ingredients. This period also saw chimneys added to many houses as central hearths were replaced with fireplaces against the wall, with more controlled heat and even specialist ovens to the sides. By the seventeenth century cast-iron pots became more common, and in the eighteenth century stoves and ranges started to be widely adopted. Skillets lost their legs, and handles became shorter, like a modern saucepan, as the cook could stand closer to the more controlled stove. All these changes were seen first in wealthier and urban households. Cooking over an open fire was still common for the poorest into the nineteenth century, and for more transient populations and those working away from home, like hop pickers and railway navvies.

Side view of the skillet, showing the rough, sooted, outer face compared to the glossy interior and the broken handle with a missing leg below, on the left (NARC-3775C7).

31

Toy cauldrons were popular and show how long the legs could be before being worn and broken. Lugs on each side allowed cauldrons to be hung over the fire. Found in Knayton with Brawith, North Yorkshire, 31 mm high (NCL-4A1286).

Reconstruction of open hearth cooking, showing a similar shaped iron skillet being used to cook vegetables over a pile of embers raked from the main fire. (Courtesy of Virginia State Park)

14. Copper-alloy pocket sundial (IOW-EA5F72)
1575–1800
Found in Brading, Isle of Wight, in 2008. Diameter 39 mm.

These sundials are known as ring, or pocket, dials. They are formed of a ring with a slot on one side, flanked by letters: I (for J, January) to I (June) below, and I (July) to D (December) above. The sliding collar running around the middle would be set into position for the month of the year; at the moment it is set to October. When the dial was suspended, the sun would shine through the hole in the collar onto the ring's interior, lighting up the hour marks. On the exterior, opposite the months, is inscribed: 'As time and hours pass away / So doth life of man decay'.

Such dials were designed to work around central England and would become more inaccurate further north. The close-set numbers would also make it hard to be more accurate than to the half or maybe quarter hour in the middle of the day. People familiar with their local landscape, and the journey of the sun across it, might be able to make a similar estimate. Buying a manufactured pocket sundial might allow the owner to feel a part of, and show off, scientific understanding of time and new discoveries in astronomy. Such understanding was also tied into ideas of control over nature and, by extension, people.

These dials became fashionable in the late sixteenth century, about the same time as pocket watches. Unlike early watches, dials were affordable even to those of only middling wealth and probably about as accurate. Through the seventeenth and eighteenth centuries clock and watch making improved and they became more affordable. By the nineteenth century, faster means of communication, particularly the railways, made knowing the time to the minute more important. It also became important to standardise midday to be the same time everywhere; sundials show midday when the sun is directly overhead, which happens at a different time when you are in western or eastern England.

Pocket sundial (IOW-EA5F72).

Pocket watches in the shape of something else were fashionable in the first half of the eighteenth century. Oswald Durant, the maker of this shell-shaped watch, was active from 1731 to 1745. Found in Nash, Buckinghamshire, 47 mm long (BUC-7A4E6C).

The watch's mechanism – the hinge allowed this to be lifted out of the separate case.

15. Copper-alloy prosthetic nose (SUSS-05BC17)
1500–1700
Found in Beddingham, East Sussex, and recorded in 2010. Length 45 mm.

This finely moulded metal nose has holes at the side to allow it to be tied onto the head, and nostril slits for breathing at the base. It was probably worn by someone who had lost their nose due to accident or illness. Syphilis can lead to loss of the nose and was widespread in the post-medieval period.

Tycho Brahe, the Danish astronomer (1546–1601), famously had a silver nose as he had lost his real one in a duel. When his grave was excavated in 1901 copper staining was found on the skull and it was suggested he had an 'everyday' nose of copper as well. A nose very similar to this example was illustrated in a sixteenth-century collection of writings on medicine and surgery, and some more modern examples, in painted silver, are in museums.

This copper-alloy example would have been quite heavy to wear all the time, but would have protected the damaged area as well as slightly disguising the loss. Like the museum examples, it may have originally been painted to make it more realistic.

Copper-alloy
prosthetic nose
(SUSS-05BC17).

16. Salt-glazed ceramic toilet bowl (SUR-146F10)
1880–1901
Found in Frimley Green, Surrey, in 2005. Length 510 mm.

In late nineteenth- and early twentieth-century Britain new medicines and vaccines saved many lives but it was good sanitation, personal hygiene and clean water that made the largest difference to life expectancy. Flushing toilets, using streams and, later, piped water, are as old as the Neolithic, but in the late eighteenth century the development of the S-bend made toilets much more sanitary and reduced the smell. As new sewerage systems spread in Victorian towns, toilets started to be mass produced and became much more common and affordable.

This 'washout' style toilet bowl was made by Doultons of London. Poo would land on an interior shelf where you could inspect it, before washing it out with water flushed from the back. Today we might associate Royal Doulton with fine china plates and figurines, but in 1845 Henry Doulton decided to invest in the new sanitary revolution, becoming a world leader in glazed stoneware drain and sewer pipe production. By the 1870s Doultons were making water filters, sinks, toilets and other goods for the growing market.

This is a freestanding toilet of the type developed in the 1880s; before that toilet bowls were fitted into wooden boxes with metal waste pipes. It is not the functional, sleek, usually white, design we are used to. It is decorated and elaborate, probably for an indoor bathroom, which in the late nineteenth century was still a middle- and upper-class luxury.

Toilet bowl (SUR-146F10). The S-bend would have attached to the pipe at the front and formed a foot for the bowl.

17. Gold mourning ring (NMS-6AA818)
1662
Found near Attleborough, Norfolk, in 2013. Diameter 23 mm.

In the sixteenth and seventeenth centuries people often left money in their wills for clothes, or just gloves, to family, friends, or local people who were poor. These would be worn for the funeral procession but were also reusable and valuable. By the later seventeenth century leaving money for finger-rings became popular – these had a commemorative but also financial value. During the eighteenth century these mourning rings became more focussed on commemoration, and by the nineteenth century there was a wide range of mourning jewellery, some incorporating the hair of the deceased (see Find 9).

Seventeenth-century mourning rings often featured a skull, as on this example, or even a full skeleton. This ring commemorated Hugh Audley of Buckenham, Norfolk, and the Inner Temple, London, who died on 15 November 1662; this date and his name are inscribed on the inner face. Audley was a very rich and well-known money lender; his death was noted by Samuel Pepys in his diary. Hugh Audley's will is in the National Archives and directs at least eleven rings be made, specifying £10 per ring for family and £5 for friends. Given the simplicity of the ring the legacies may have been expected to leave money over for clothes and gloves. Ten pounds was almost five months' wages for a skilled craftsman at this time and other wills indicate amounts as low as 20 shillings (£1) could buy a ring.

Mourning ring with skull commemorating Hugh Audley of Buckenham, Norfolk (d. 1662) (NMS-6AA818).

This later, eighteenth-century, ring has the names on the outside; it is more valuable, with a rock crystal or glass setting, more individual and more personal. It commemorates Mary and Sarah Littleton. Mary died giving birth to her daughter, Sarah, who was christened immediately, showing she was not expected to live. Sarah died the next day, 7 June 1735. It was probably made for Thomas Littleton, husband of Mary and father of Sarah. Found in Bridgnorth, Shropshire, 23 mm in diameter (HESH-E35784).

Play and Leisure

In traditional histories play and recreation might seem a minor component, with the past appearing very serious, or even brutal, but play, and toys, are universal throughout history. Toys are scattered through this book as they reflect many aspects of people's lives, and, of course, the ways people play reflect wider social and economic factors. Some of the objects below, such as dolls and tankards, may feel completely familiar. This period also saw a lot of change, including the widespread availability of distilled liquor and imported drinks, the introduction of tobacco to Europe, the decline of sports such as hawking and hunting with dogs and the codification of games and sports with set equipment and spaces.

Image of a Dutch country fair painted between 1680 and 1704. (*Country Kermis* by Cornelis Dusart, courtesy of the Rijksmuseum, Amsterdam)

18. Silver and enamel hawking vervel (HESH-A49557)
1500–55
Found in South Herefordshire in 2007. Length 20 mm.

Keeping birds of prey and hunting with them has long been a marker of elite leisure time and social interaction. The activity also highlighted distinctions within the elite, through the different types of bird thought appropriate for different social ranks – from the king's gyrfalcon to the kestrel for a knave. Much of our knowledge of hawking comes from documentary evidence; most of the organic evidence – such as leather leashes and hoods – has been lost, while artefacts like small bells can have many uses and so can be hard to associate firmly with hawking. An exception is provided by the 'vervel', an object we now know a lot more about through the recording of detector finds.

Hawking vervel (HESH-A49557).

Vervels are small metal tags mostly attached to jesses – leather straps that connected a hawk's legs to its leash. They functioned as identification labels, often being engraved with an owner's name and residence. This shield-shaped form is rare, most vervels being simple washer-like rings. Its enamelled ground surrounding a rampant lion is also an indicator of its higher cost. The inscription, 'T/ NOR/FOC/K', seems to relate to the Dukes of Norfolk. The second, third, fourth, fifth and eighth Dukes were all called Thomas. The silver (white) lion on a red background was part of the duke's arms, alluding to their descent from the Mowbray family. It was replaced in 1555 with a gold lion for FitzAlan, marking the fourth duke's marriage, so this vervel should be no later than that. Interestingly, a very similar vervel has been found near Witham, Essex (ESS-D74C32), testifying to the extensive travels and connections of the dukes.

This annular (ring-shaped) vervel asks the bird's finder to 'Returne to Gilbert Hody / of Alscot in Devon'. Alscot is a phonetic spelling of Alverdiscott (West Devon); the vervel was found nearly 50 miles away near Ottery St Mary, illustrating the social status and connections of Hody, who lived at Alscot between the 1640s and 1680s. 14 mm in diameter (DEV-6141DD).

19. Ceramic beer or wine bottle (SUR-CDA28E)
1595
Found in Bagshot, Surrey, in 2017. Weight 368 g.

This bottle would have been used to transport liquids, and serve wine or beer at the table. It was made in modern-day Germany out of a very hard stoneware ceramic with a mottled salt-glaze. Such bottles were very popular from the late sixteenth century and through the seventeenth. They have been found all over the world, from a shipwreck in Western Australia to the graves of indigenous inhabitants in colonial North America. On the neck is a cheerful, bearded face with the bottle providing the round bellied 'body'. This style is known as a Bartmann (bearded man) or Bellarmine jug. Cardinal Robert Bellarmine was a learned and influential anti-Reformation teacher; his catechism, a teaching aid, has been translated into sixty languages. His name became attached to these jugs in seventeenth-century Protestant areas as an insult – he was well known to be against drinking alcohol.

Such bottles, and glass wine bottles, were expensive and reused many times. They could be taken to the local brewer or wine merchant for refilling. Wine bottles often had a glass seal applied; this helped them to be returned to the right owner and showed others you could afford personalised bottles. The heraldic seal on the side of this jug, which is flanked by a date, 1595, is purely decorative. Jugs were produced with the arms of local German nobility or with completely made up heraldry.

Beer or wine bottle (SUR-CDA28E).

Sixteenth-century wooden tankard with iron bands and owner's initials on the base, missing its hinged lid. It could have held three pints so was probably shared or used as a decanter. Similar, but smaller, tankards have been found on the wreck of the *Mary Rose* (sank 1545); they were found in different parts of the ship, suggesting they were used by all classes of sailors. Found on the Thames foreshore in London, 220 mm high (LON-AAED92).

20. Lead-alloy toy pot hanger (LON-041F02)
1650–1700
Found on the Thames foreshore in London, in 2012. Length 72 mm.

Small toys from the sixteenth to nineteenth centuries are often made of lead alloys, as they were cheap, easy to cast into elaborate shapes, and could be melted even on a domestic fire. Adding a bit of tin to the lead made them lighter, harder and shinier. These toys often copy objects of the time and some may have been played with in doll's houses. Not just children had dolls' houses; in the late seventeenth and early eighteenth century there was a fashion amongst wealthy women for very elaborate ones with silver furniture.

This is an elaborate, decorated, and very delicate model of a pot hanger. Pot hangers were iron devices that were fixed over a fire. This example includes an adjustable ring ratchet on the saw-toothed bar – a development that became popular in the early seventeenth century. It meant the hanging pots could be raised or lowered easily, making cooking over an open hearth safer.

Toy pot hanger, perhaps once used in a doll's house's fireplace (LON-041F02).

Right: Toys are often presumed to be contemporary with the larger objects they copy. The form of this gridiron, used to grill a fish over a fire, suggests a sixteenth- or early seventeenth-century date, but it was found under the floorboards of a house built in 1861 with a marble, some slate pencils and other broken objects. Found in Woolpit, Suffolk, 66 mm long (FAHG-C743A5).

Below: This late sixteenth-century elaborate 3D model of a coach and horses was made of several pieces that the owner could fold and put together themselves. The horse's head, the roof and one set of wheels are missing, as is probably a foil or fabric liner. The coach is of a wagon-like form popular at the time but highly embellished, like those of the aristocracy. Found on the Thames foreshore in London, 65 mm long (LON-81D1C7).

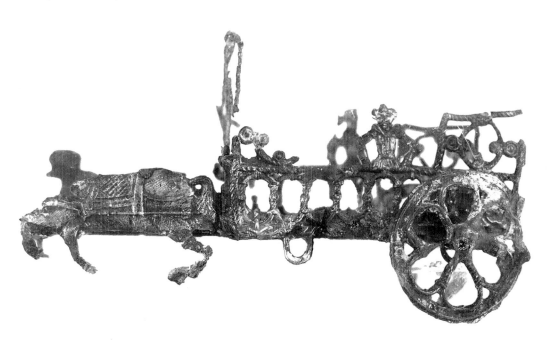

21. Copper-alloy dog collar (SOM-DAD21E)
1676–80
Found in Ashcott, Somerset, in 2016. Diameter 164 mm.

The collar is inscribed 'Samuell Birch (shield of arms) att Shilton neare Burford in Oxfordshir[e 1]676'. The overlapping ends were held by an iron fitting, which also attached to a swivel for the leash. The size of the collar suggests that it was worn by a large-necked hunting dog. All-metal collars seem to be a broadly seventeenth-century fashion, one replaced in the eighteenth century by leather collars with metal plaques. The metal collars would have been very showy, in shining metal, but heavy and probably uncomfortable for the dog. They may have been taken off when the dog was released to chase.

Samuel Birch (1620–80) was born in Manchester and studied at Oxford University. He was a major in the Parliamentarian army where he fought under his brother John, a colonel. After the Civil War, Samuel became a minister, but at the Restoration in 1660 he refused to follow the reinstated Church of England services and teachings and was ejected from his parish. In 1664 he moved to Shilton where he opened a 'conventicling' school for sons of Dissenters, which proved very popular. In his religious beliefs he was a learned and fervent Puritan but the collar shows a different side, someone who enjoyed hunting, and had a dog he was proud of. He was presumably visiting Somerset when the collar, and perhaps his dog, was lost in this marshy area, sometime between 1676 and his death in 1680.

Angled view to show the collar's whole shape with the legend transcribed below (SOM-DAD21E).

Detail from an Italian plate of 1610 depicting a huntsman and a dog wearing a similar collar. Now in the Musée national Adrien Dubouché, Limoges. (Image by authors)

22. Lead buzz disc (PUBLIC-296871)
1650–1800
Found in Tenterden, Kent, in 2014. Diameter 31 mm.

In contrast to the finely made toys on the last few pages, this simple buzz disc or 'whirligig' was probably homemade, cut from a piece of lead sheet. It would be hung on strings running through the holes in the centre and could be wound up by swinging the disc around. When the strings were pulled tight the disc would spin rapidly. The air rushing past the toothed edge would make a loud buzz. It may have been simple but it was obviously cared for; the owner has marked it with their initials, 'E M'.

Lead buzz disc marked with its owner's initials (PUBLIC-296871).

Musical instruments rarely survive as finds. We can learn more about their form and popularity from other objects, such as this knife handle, which shows a man playing the bagpipes, with a hunting horn tucked into his belt at the back. Probably made in the Netherlands, it was found in Kettering, Northamptonshire, 73 mm long (NARC-D89036).

23. Copper-alloy pipe tamper (BERK-32983C)
1700–50
Found in Cassington, Oxfordshire, in 2017. Length 73 mm.

Consumption of tobacco, by smoking or as snuff, was a mainstay of post-medieval society that developed from the late sixteenth century onwards. Tobacco is an important part of the colonial history of the period and offers both global and local insights into trade and consumption patterns. Archaeological evidence for smoking is offered primarily by clay pipes, but associated paraphernalia is also found: snuff boxes, pipe tongs, and even trade tokens relating to the sale of tobacco or pipes.

A type of metal object brought to the fore through PAS evidence is the pipe stopper, or tamper. From the early seventeenth century onwards, these were used to maintain the correct density of tobacco in the bowl for effective smoking. Many designs have been documented, including political, satirical and bawdy ones, as well as the more prosaic. This example actually takes the form of smoking equipment: a pair of long-stemmed pipes held in a decorative frame. A detachable pick completes the ensemble and would have been used both for cleaning pipe stems and aerating tobacco in the bowl. Pipe bowl forms and stem lengths changed through time, dating this tamper to the early 1700s.

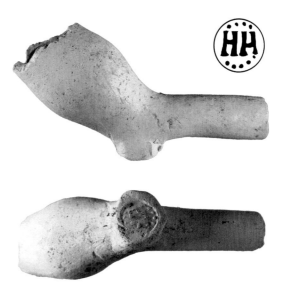

Above: On the heel of the bowl of this incomplete clay tobacco pipe is a previously undocumented maker's mark of 'H H'. The bowl shape suggests a date between 1620 and 1660. Closely dated objects like this have great potential for reconstructing local industries and patterns of trade. Found in Yoxall, Staffordshire, now 57 mm long (WMID-F58075).

Left: Eighteenth-century pipe tamper depicting a pair of long-stemmed smoking pipes (BERK-32983C).

24. Ivory token or pass (KENT-791E68)
1697–1758
Found on the Thames foreshore in London, in 2018. Diameter 28 mm.

Lambeth Wells, the name written on this token, was in Three Coney Walk (now Lambeth Walk) in London. Originally the 'wells' were mineral water springs, of a type also found in spa towns such as Bath, Tunbridge Wells and Harrogate. Drinking the water was thought to be purging and to cure various ills. Bottled waters were sold from the site and by 1697 there was a 'Great Hall' used for music, dancing and lectures. The entrance fee was 3*d*, or one shilling for special events. This token was probably given to visitors at the entrance and redeemed for refreshments or entry to a show.

Lambeth Wells was never as popular or fashionable as the contemporary Vauxhall Gardens; and by 1758 it was decried as nothing more than a 'nuisance and a common brothel'. It soon lost its dancing licence, though it continued in use as tea gardens for some time. In the nineteenth century the building was rebuilt as a pub, the Fountain, and a small open space remained of the previous fields, called Fountain Gardens. After bomb damage in the Second World War the entire area, which had become very poor, was redeveloped as housing. Fountain Gardens were incorporated into Lambeth Walk Open Space and 300 years later remain an area for retreat and refreshment from city living.

Ivory token or pass from Lambeth Wells, London (KENT-791E68).

A fashionable couple of 1830 take a romantic walk in a similar pleasure garden. (Courtesy of the British Library, London/Unsplash)

25. Lead-alloy doll (DUR-2F2D86)
1700–1800
Found in Loftus, Redcar and Cleveland, in 2009. Length 58 mm.

Dolls have been popular as children's toys for thousands of years. In the sixteenth to eighteenth centuries, as well as wooden and china dolls, lead 'flats' were made. These were cast in an open-top or two-sided mould and show women in elaborate court dresses, or men, often on horseback. As well as being played, and play acted, with in the same way children do with dolls today, the looped arms with hands at the hip allowed them to be 'walked' between people on strings. Models of animals, typically a cockerel, could also be stood up and used as 'shys' where you threw an object at them, scoring points if they fell over. Male dolls were often shown outfitted as soldiers or hunters, whereas this smiling figure just seems to be riding. He has very large, prominent coat buttons, similar to Find 7. This type of flat doll is more common in north-east England and was probably made locally.

Horserider doll, the back of which is flat and plain (DUR-2F2D86).

This crudely made female doll wears an elaborate dress with blobby jewels and a large upstanding collar, fashionable around 1600–25. On the back is a similar but less dressed image, perhaps allowing for clothes to be added over the underskirt in the same way as paper dolls today. Found in Healeyfield, County Durham, 93 mm high (NCL-DB1E00).

Eighteenth- or nineteenth-century cast lead owl with a broken base which may have been used as a 'shy'. Found in Plumley, Cheshire East, 40 mm in width (LVPL-555B72).

We can understand the other finds in this book through texts, the places they are found in and by comparison with other examples. For very modern discoveries, like these medals, living people can sometimes flesh out the story behind the find. These five medals were found together on the Thames foreshore. Remarkably, they all originated from the famous Wimbledon Tennis Championships and had all been awarded to American player Peter Fleming. Fleming enjoyed a particularly successful doubles career, notably alongside John McEnroe, in the late 1970s and early 1980s. While they won the Wimbledon doubles championships together four times, these medals relate to five slightly less successful tournaments. They all come from occasions when Fleming and his partner were runners-up or semi-finalists.

While we may allow ourselves to speculate that this was Fleming throwing out reminders of his less successful tournaments, such a suggestion cannot be serious. In fact, Fleming reported to the PAS that he had been the victim of a burglary a few years previously. Of the material stolen, any object traceable to him was jettisoned along the riverbank, including an engraved watch found near Putney Bridge. Happily, the medals have been reunited with their winner.

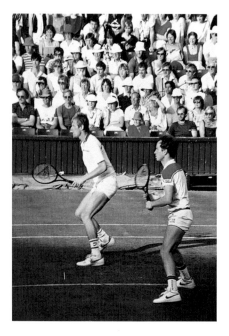

Above: The earliest of the recovered Wimbledon medals, awarded in 1978 (LON-7A617B).

Left: Peter Fleming (left) playing doubles at Wimbledon with John McEnroe in the 1980s. (Image via Wikimedia Commons)

Religion

Religion and belief were really important forces in people's lives throughout this period. Conflict between those who held different beliefs and wanted different practices within Christianity arose particularly in the sixteenth to eighteenth centuries – not just between Protestants and Catholics during the Reformation in the sixteenth century, but also between different reforming movements within Protestantism. This religious strife was a key issue for individuals concerned with their own souls, within communities, and nationally, shaping politics and international relations. An acceptance of non-uniformity in Christian belief across England and Wales gradually developed from the eighteenth century, and has now come to embrace official acceptance of other faiths. This is a very different attitude to the legal persecution, missionary activity and use of religious difference to justify invasion, occupation and colonialism that we see from the British state through most of this period. Private and non-official beliefs and practices have always run alongside organised religion. Compared to a history of religion told through buildings or printed texts, it seems that the lost, discarded or hidden objects featured here are particularly good at telling the stories of personal, non-official, minority and even persecuted beliefs.

The familiar form of St Paul's in London was a result of the cathedral's complete redesign and rebuilding after the fire of 1666. (Image by Andrea De Santis/ Unsplash)

27. Copper-alloy pilgrim badge (NMS-3D99F3)
1475–1525
Found in Morningthorpe, Norfolk, in 2017. Diameter 30 mm.

This looks like a button, but rather than fastening clothing it was a badge which could be pinned or sewn onto clothes or a hat. It is of a type known as a 'bouton-enseigne', with most examples found in north-east France. They are made of a silvery looking copper alloy. This eight-lobed example depicts St Nicholas and the 'three boys in a brine-tub'.

Tradition has it that an evil shopkeeper in the town of Myra (now in Turkey) hated children so he kidnapped three small boys, chopped them up with an axe, and pickled them in a barrel. Nicholas, the local bishop, upon hearing of this horror, prayed fervently to God. The boys were raised to life and came out of the pickle barrel singing 'Alleluia!'. Several legends surround St Nicholas's care for children and his secret gift giving, which may be why he is now better known as Santa Claus (Father Christmas).

In the decades before the English Reformation (1530s) the nature of western Christianity was changing. An emphasis on pilgrimage and collective worship in the medieval period was giving way to an emotional devotion to individual saints and a focus on personal acts and prayers. While this object is still called a 'pilgrim badge', it need not have been purchased on pilgrimage to a shrine. The detailed design, rather than the clear outline of earlier badges, would be most visible to the wearer, or those close to them – a reminder and focus of contemplation on the saint, and their story.

Drawing of the 'button' badge (NMS-3D99F3).

28. Copper-alloy purse bar (KENT-BB3F94)
1450–1550
Found in Istead Rise, Kent, in 2017. Length 173 mm.

In the late fifteenth and early sixteenth century there was a fashion for large leather or cloth purses with a shining metal top bar and frame. Each of this purse bar's arms has a tab on the lower edge with sewing holes to attach the bag. The arms bear the inscription, 'AVE MA/ G[R]ACIA' on one face and '[P]LENA D/NS TECV' on the other, a contraction of the phrase 'Ave Maria Gracia Plena, Dominus Tecum' ('Hail Mary, full of grace, the Lord is with you'). The phrase is derived from the angel Gabriel's greeting to Mary and was used in a prayer as part of the rosary. Contractions of the phrase were popular on purse bars and other personal and domestic items in the period before the religious Reformation of the mid-sixteenth century.

This bar is very unusual in that on its central boss is a small portrait of a young male in late medieval or Tudor garb. Both the portrait and inscription are executed with inlaid niello (a silver and sulphur compound). The portrait is flanked by the letters V and I, with a possible letter above the V. It appears to be of Henry VI (1422–61; 1470–71) or Edward VI (1547–53). While the pointed face and wide decorated hat is similar to portraits of Edward VI, bars of this type appear to have fallen out of fashion before his reign started. Furthermore, the combination of an inscription associated with Catholic worship and the fervently Protestant Edward VI would be highly unusual. A portrayal of Henry VI, king and martyr, possibly wearing a decorative collar of the order of the Golden Fleece, therefore seems more likely. Henry VI was the Lancastrian king whose deposition sparked the Wars of the Roses. His cult was not officially recognised by the church but was promoted by his Lancastrian successor Henry VII in the late fifteenth and early sixteenth century.

The full bar with suspension loop to hang from a belt (KENT-BB3F94).

Above: Close up of the central boss.

Left: Detail showing the large purse worn by Thomas White in his tomb effigy, St Mary's Church, Tenby. (Image by authors)

29. Lead papal bulla (SUR-F847F3)
1555–59
Found in Odiham, Hampshire, in 2016. Diameter 38 mm.

While the oldest papal bulla recorded by the PAS dates from the turn of the eighth century, this example is the most modern currently known from Britain. Bullae were lead seals attached to papal documents, called 'bulls', to guarantee their genuine status, just as wax seals might be used on other documents (see Find 9). Holes can be seen at the top and bottom where a silk or hemp cord once passed through the bulla, for attachment to the vellum. The design is standardised, with the pope's name on the front – identifying this as issued by Paul IV (1555–59). The reverse features the heads of Saints Peter and Paul, as bullae had since the late eleventh century. This more naturalistic portrait style was adopted in the late fifteenth century, influenced by Renaissance art. This is currently the only bulla on the PAS database from after the start of the English Reformation. It may be associated with the nation's brief return to the Roman Catholic Church under Mary I.

Above: Papal bulla of Paul IV (SUR-F847F3).

Right: Papal order (bull) of 1527 with a similar bulla attached at the bottom. (Courtesy of the Jagiellonian Digital Library, Krakow/Europeana)

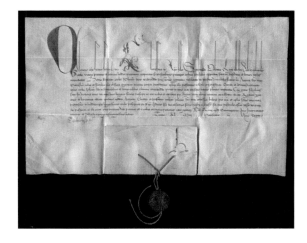

30. Lead 'decade' ring (DUR-36116F)
1550–1700
Found in Brough with St Giles, North Yorkshire, in 2019. Diameter 36 mm.

This rather crude finger-ring has ten globular protrusions on its exterior and a bezel that shows Christ crucified. These features are counting aids, like a rosary – sets of beads moved between the fingers to keep track of the number of prayers said. The ten protrusions – hence 'decade' ring – relate to the 'Hail Mary' prayers (the 'Ave Maria'), while the bezel prompted the 'Lord's Prayer' (the 'Pater Noster').

These rings are more commonly recorded on the PAS database than wood or bone rosary beads, which decay in the soil. While decade rings are known from the fourteenth century onwards, many, such as this example, are thought to be expressions of continued Catholic devotion after the Reformation. Traditional practices, including using a rosary and saying the Latin Mass, were made illegal and termed 'recusancy'; they could lead to fines, imprisonment and death. The rings are a more discreet attachment to Catholic ritual, important following the prohibition of rosaries in 1571. As well as being cheap and easy to cast with little equipment, these rings were also easy to melt down on a hearth fire if they needed to be concealed.

Lead decade ring showing crucifixion on the projecting bezel (DUR-36116F).

As stray finds, rosary beads can be difficult to identify due to their plainness. This unusually large and distinctive sixteenth-century wooden example may have been the rosary's primary bead – for the Pater – akin to the bezel on a decade ring. The skull depicted served as a reminder of mortality, or 'memento mori'. Found on the Thames foreshore in London, 27 mm high (LON-78B66F).

Decade rings are found across England and Wales but these distinctive leaden examples seem to be concentrated in the north and, to a lesser extent, the Midlands. These areas also saw continued resistance to the end of Catholicism in the sixteenth century, including the rebellion known as the Pilgrimage of Grace in 1536.

This monstrance, of 1550–1650, would have been used to elevate and display the consecrated communion wafer during the mass, a practice made illegal in 1559. While elaborately decorated, it is made in cheap pewter and is much smaller than the usual gold or silver monstrances. Like the decade rings it could be concealed or quickly broken up and melted to hide illegal Catholic practices. Found on the Thames foreshore in London, 62 mm high (LON-976376).

Using a pyx to store communion wafers for use with the sick and dying was also made illegal in 1559. This seventeenth-century silver pyx depicts the crucifixion on the front and Christ as the sacrificial Lamb of God on the reverse. The front reads: 'VINCENTI DABO EI MANNA ABSCONDITUM', a verse from the biblical Book of Revelation. This means: 'To him that overcomes I will give the hidden manna' – an extremely suitable verse for the secret pyx of a persecuted Catholic. Found near Preston, Lancashire, 53 mm in diameter (LANCUM-6F19D5).

31. Silver apostle spoon terminal (LVPL-883FF2)
1500–1660
Found in Bawtry, Nottinghamshire, in 2011. Height 32 mm.

Silver spoons, sometimes gilded, with the end of the handle shaped into a figure of one of the twelve apostles, or of Jesus or Mary, were popular from around 1470 to 1660. Simpler types with more generic figures continued to be made into the twentieth century. They were commonly given as christening gifts – a full set by the wealthy or just one spoon if that was all that could be afforded. Cheaper examples also exist in copper alloys and in pewter.

This figure holds a long, jagged saw by his left leg and a book or tablet in his right hand. The saw suggests it is the apostle Simon Zelotes, who is said to have been martyred by being sawn in half. He is the patron saint of sawyers, following the medieval trend of assigning saints as patrons of jobs that use the tools the saint was killed by.

End of a spoon handle with attachment hole at the base (LVPL-883FF2).

Religious inscriptions remained common on household objects in this period. Compared to medieval examples they are more likely to be in English and appeal for personal devotion and good behaviour rather than to the saint's intercession. Seventeenth-century silver thimble inscribed 'FARE (fear) GOD' found near Colchester, Essex, 27 mm high (ESS-723482).

Bible stories and characters were also widely used in domestic decoration and on objects, like this seventeenth-century knife handle depicting Jonah rising from the Whale. It was probably made in the Low Countries but was found in Barley, Hertfordshire, 76 mm long (BH-8D8C03).

32. Lead dreidel spinner (IOW-918A57)
1700–1900
Found on the Isle of Wight, in 2007. Length 23 mm.

Dreidels are toy spinners used in a game where, depending on your spin, you either took out or added money or tokens to a central pot. On each side the spinner has a letter in the Hebrew alphabet that told the player what to do: Nun (nit, nothing), Gimel (gants, take all), Hey (halb, take half), Shin (shtel, put one in). This is a variant on a game which has existed for thousands of years; Roman dreidel have been found in England. Playing with dreidel became a custom for Jewish families at Hanukkah.

Hanukkah is celebrated in late November or December and commemorates the rededication of the Temple by the Maccabees. When they regained the temple after a revolt only one day's supply of holy oil was left untouched. This miraculously burned for eight days, the time it took to make new oil. Menorah candle holders, with eight lights, are traditionally lit over the eight-day holiday to commemorate this great miracle. The Hebrew letters in the dreidel can also be read as the initials of the phrase 'Nes Gadol Haya Sham' (a Great Miracle Happened There).

In England, after the widespread massacres and expulsion of Jewish inhabitants in the thirteenth century, there was no open Jewish presence until the law was changed in 1656 by Oliver Cromwell to allow people of Jewish faith to settle here. Small communities soon formed, especially in cities that traded with the Continent. This type of spinner was popular in Germany, but, being simply cast out of lead, it may have been made locally. Other material remains of British Jewish communities include seal matrices and seals for marking Kosher food, prepared according to religious laws.

Lead dreidel spinner (IOW-918A57).

An eighteenth- or nineteenth-century lead kosher seal. One disc has Hebrew letters: אבד (ABD, or av bet din ('Chief of the (Rabbinical) Court')) and דכק (DKK, or de kehillah kedosha ('of the Holy Community')). The other disc has partial letters א[...], which probably relate to the specific supplier. Found on the Thames foreshore in London, 43 mm long (SUR-69A253).

33. Possible 'witch bottle' (LIN-49FC12)
1820–80
Found in Navenby, Lincolnshire, in 2003. Height *c.* 55 mm.

When this decorative glass inkwell or candle holder was found under the floorboards of a house it contained a mass of corroded iron, with a strip of leather, bent pins and dress hooks. There are historical records in the seventeenth and eighteenth centuries of sealed pottery vessels, and, later, glass containers being placed in houses, often under entrances which could be 'vulnerable', like a doorway or hearthstone. The containers were filled with varying quantities of bent nails, cloth, human hair, fingernail clippings and urine. These 'witch bottles' were protective, diverting spells aimed at the house and occupants to the container, or even actively throwing evil spells back on the witch who cast them. This object is particularly interesting as the glass is mould blown suggesting it is no earlier than 1820, later than other accounts of this practice. By this point the ritual may have been more personal and varied and the depositor may have hoped to repel bad luck or ill wishing more generally.

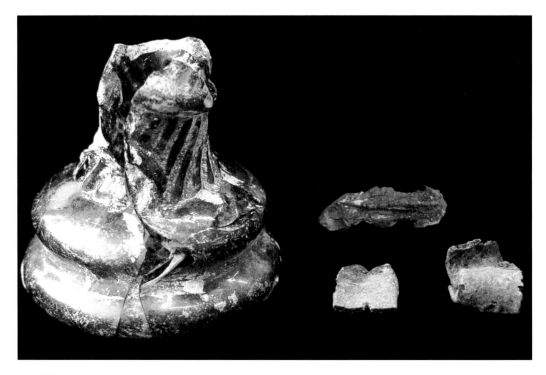

Possible 'witch bottle' and some of its contents (LIN-49FC12).

Child's shoe, only 110 mm long, found in a chimney in Ewerby, Lincolnshire, with a miniature bible dating to 1901 (LIN-121483). Shoes and other clothing are often found concealed in buildings. Old shoes mould to the individual foot of the wearer, so like the fingernails, hair and urine mentioned, might retain some of their wearer's spirit or could represent them. The bible might have been intended to destroy any evil attracted to the shoe, showing such practices could be combined with Christian material.

34. Stone shiva 'lingam' or 'Shivling' (LIN-A784E5)
1980–2017
Found in Skegness, Lincolnshire, in 2017. Height 71 mm.

Found on the beach at Skegness, this greenstone object is an abstract representation of the Hindu deity Shiva, known as a 'lingam' (Sanskrit for 'symbol'). Shiva lingams or 'Shivlings' can occur as natural objects, such as domed stones, or as votive models used for worship in temples or smaller shrines. They are considered sacred by devotees. This item was probably recently deposited at the ocean's edge and had not travelled far up the coast before it was found; it has neither broken nor become very sea-worn. Depositions into water are used in many religions and other objects of Hindu association have been found nearby, including another lingam found in Cleethorpes (SWYOR-3670C3).

After its discovery, the Lincolnshire Finds Liaison Officer took this lingam to the local Hindu Cultural Society. They explained that its deposition possibly related to the owner no longer being able to carry out the rituals required for its worship, perhaps due to ill health. Since Hindu custom forbids destruction of these items, one of the appropriate methods of disposal is to put it in the sea to let the gods take care of it.

Shiva 'lingam' or 'Shivling' (LIN-A784E5).

Nineteenth-century Indian painting showing a woman, possibly Bhairavi Ragini, putting a garland around the Shivling while the others pray. (Courtesy of the Wellcome Collection, London/Europeana)

This modern Islamic silver amulet was also deposited into water; it was found wrapped in this well used leather pouch and then a plastic bag. It has a verse from the Quran and a magic square referencing the ninety-nine names of God. Found on the Thames foreshore in London, 29 mm in diameter (SUR-B3656D).

War

Metal-detecting evidence can be very important in identifying the location and events of military clashes, usually through the detailed mapping of types of shot and small objects like buttons. However, most of the finds in this chapter don't reflect big battles or the political or military leaders in war. Many were nothing to do with the fighting itself, but show the influence of war – even wars fought overseas – on everyday life in England and Wales. From toys to novelty goods and clothing, many consumer goods show the influence of wars on the imagination or demonstrate support for regimes and leaders. Even military goods highlighted below, such as the helmet and sword, were probably used for display longer than they were for fighting. Finds from a Second World War prisoner-of-war camp highlight the everyday life of soldiers, as well as the mass production and standardised goods issued to them in an industrial age.

In Europe much of what we associate with an army now – uniforms, guns, marching in formation and training as units – was introduced in this period. *Column on the March, 1915*, by Christopher Richard W. Nevinson. (Courtesy of the Birmingham Museums Trust/ Unsplash)

35. Iron cannon ball (CORN-508D86)
1595
Found at Paul, Cornwall, in 2015. Diameter 68 mm.

On 2 August 1595 four Spanish galleons carrying 400 men sailed into Mount's Bay in West Cornwall. They landed men near the small port of Mousehole, which they attacked from the shore, and bombarded from the ships. A second group climbed the hill above to attack the village of Paul. Four residents of Paul were killed, others captured, and the church was burned. This cannon ball is one of several found near the church over the years and probably broke in half on impact.

The next day the Spanish sailed around the bay, attacking and burning houses in Newlyn and Penzance. After defeating a local militia at Penzance they celebrated mass in a field, promising to return and build a church on the spot when the whole of England was conquered. This raid was the only invasion of England during the Anglo-Spanish War of 1585–1604. After the disaster of the Spanish Armada in 1588, and the failure of the retaliatory English Armada, King Philip II of Spain reorganised his navy, founding a strong base in Brittany from which to harass English shipping and launch raids like this one on Cornwall.

Right: Broken cannon ball (CORN-508D86).

Below: Mount's Bay, Cornwall, with St Michael's Mount in the foreground and beyond the mount, Mousehole, with the village of Paul on the headland above. (Image by Benjamin Elliott/Unsplash)

This helmet is formed of a main 'skull' of two pieces of iron, connected at the top along the comb. At the front a separate peak not only survives but can still pivot. Rivets and roves around the base of the 'skull' would have held a padded inner lining, for comfort and fit. The helmet is only otherwise missing its triple-bar faceguard and cheek-pieces. Riveted to the back is a separate neck-guard. Subtle, horizontal lines on the guard give it the appearance of separate strips, even though it is made of one piece of metal. The resemblance of the guard to a segmented lobster's tail gave these helmets the name 'lobster pot'. 'Lobster pots' were worn by harquebusiers (light cavalry) throughout much of the seventeenth century, but the exact form of this example, plus a maker's mark for London armourer Henry Keene, suggests it was made in the mid to late 1640s, during the British Civil Wars.

The level of survival of this helmet implies it was kept safe, probably on display or stored in a building, between its use in the Civil War and later deposition in the ground. While a few other 'pot' helmets have been recorded through the PAS – probably belonging to pikemen rather than cavalry – they do not survive as well. Along with far more frequently recorded munitions, such as lead musket balls, these objects help conjure this turbulent, violent period of British history.

'Lobster pot' helmet from the British Civil Wars period (LIN-E0B301).

Sword dating to around the same time. 'Andrea' is stamped on one side and 'Ferara' on the other. Andrea Ferara was a famous sword maker in the sixteenth century, and during the sixteenth and seventeenth centuries, many swords – whether made by him or not – were stamped with his name as a mark of good quality. Found in Christow, Devon, 730 mm long (DEV-BB4AF7).

37. Copper-alloy dress fastener (WAW-70FFB2)
1649–60
Found in Upton-upon-Severn, Worcestershire, in 2010. Length 35 mm.

This fastener has three small sewing loops, plus, at one end, a larger, rectangular 'eye'. Such fasteners would have been used with a corresponding piece whose blunt hook engaged with the eye. They are thought to have been used instead of buttons down the front of jerkins or buff coats – items of military clothing. The low relief design on this example shows shields bearing the Irish harp and the Cross of St George, both within a wreath. These are the Arms of the Commonwealth (but with transposed shields) which existed between 1649 and 1660, following the execution of Charles I.

Although most objects recorded by the PAS bearing the Commonwealth Arms relate to currency and trade, such as official coins, cloth seals and trade weights, others, such as this fastener, seem to be unofficial expressions of loyalism. Where such objects appear in their greatest numbers, such as in the South West, they may be evocations of a resistant identity in what was a predominantly Royalist region.

Dress fastener with broken rectangular eye on left, showing the Commonwealth Arms (WAW-70FFB2).

Enamelled button depicting the Commonwealth Arms. The enamel on the cross should be red, and may have decayed to white. Found near Hormead, Hertfordshire, 24 mm in diameter (SF-606C13).

The 1649 trial of Charles I in Westminster Hall. The Commonwealth Arms are prominently displayed on the back wall. (Print from an account of the trial published in 1684, courtesy of the State Library of Victoria, Melbourne)

38. Copper-alloy toy cannon with carriage (SOM-D20D91)
1700–50
Found in Pitminster, Somerset, in 2010. Length 78 mm.

Military toys, soldier dolls and small cannons started to be mass produced in the seventeenth century and gained in popularity in the eighteenth. Prince Charles, later Charles II, was given toy cannons on his eighth and ninth birthdays. As befitted a prince, they were larger and grander than this example, and still survive in the Royal Armouries' collection. The gun carriage on this example is made simply of cut out pieces of copper-alloy sheet, held together by iron pins. These flimsy carriages are usually lost with only the cannon barrels surviving. These very common miniature cannons can be fired; many examples are found with the barrel blown open from misfires. Toy soldiers remained popular into the twentieth century but these cannons, perhaps sensibly, fell out of favour as a toy for children.

Toy cannon complete with carriage (SOM-D20D91).

One side of a two-part mould to cast a toy cannon. Metal moulds like this were often remelted so rarely survive. Found in Aughton, Lancashire, 110 mm long (LVPL-3C5611).

39. Copper-alloy penknife handle (YORYM-38524E)
1756–63
Found in Edington, Wiltshire, in 2015. Length 84 mm.

This handle for a folding penknife was probably made in Sheffield, a city famous for its cutlers (blade makers). The handle reads: 'I SAY FOREVER HUS'A // SUCCESS TO THE KING OF PRUSSIA'. 'Huzzah' was a popular exclamation, like 'hooray', and was also used by soldiers to raise courage for a charge. The King of Prussia celebrated on this knife was Frederick the Great, a key ally of Britain in the Seven Years War (1756–63). Many pubs were named after Frederick, but most were renamed during the First World War when Prussia, by then part of Germany, meant an enemy rather than ally.

Such a knife would have been a small luxury, bought during the war and enjoyed for a few years. It is typical of the many cheap consumer goods of the eighteenth century, objects made to serve a growing retail sector and appeal to middle-class male consumers who were spending more time writing accounts and letters and had more disposable income. Other such commemorative goods included decorative pipe tampers, rotating seal matrices, tankards, cufflinks and cheap tin medals.

Mid-eighteenth-century folding penknife (YORYM-38524E).

Cheap copper-tin medal which would have been bought or given out to members of the public to commemorate Admiral Vernon's 1739 victory at Portobelo in the War of Jenkins' Ear. As well as Portobello Road in London, Mount Vernon, George Washington's home, was named after the admiral as his brother fought in the British Navy under Vernon. Found in Granby, Nottinghamshire, 36 mm in diameter (DENO-E6557B).

This Distinguished Conduct Medal from the First World War was awarded to Sgt G. H. Humber. His name is inscribed on the edge. The *London Gazette*'s citation on the award of this medal (3 September 1919) states that Sgt Humber served with Battery A in the 38th Brigade, Royal Field Artillery. He had served in France since 1915 and had carried out 'invaluable work both as a corporal and a sergeant'. The citation states: 'He has been through all the heavy fighting in 1916, 1917 and 1918, always commanding his detachment in action with great courage and coolness, often under heavy, hostile shell-fire and great difficulties'. The Distinguished Conduct Medal was the first official award for gallantry and bravery given to regular soldiers; before that only officers were recognised. It was the second highest award, below the Victoria Cross.

George Humber was born on the Isle of Wight in 1889 and died there in 1985, aged ninety-four. Press stories about the find helped the finder and local Finds Liaison Officer make contact with Humber's family. Before their marriage Humber's wife, Bessie, lived with her family near Edenbridge, a mile from where the medal was found. Humber worked in the area briefly after the war and probably lost the medal when visiting Bessie and her family. A duplicate medal was presented to George Humber shortly before he died, twenty-four years before this original one was found.

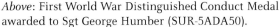

Above: First World War Distinguished Conduct Medal awarded to Sgt George Humber (SUR-5ADA50).

Right: Sgt Humber in his military uniform. (Courtesy of his family)

Six aluminium 'sporks' have been recovered from several adjacent fields in East Yorkshire. Each combines a connected spoon and fork; they pivoted at a rivet on the handle, overlapping – when not in use – with the fork's tines sitting in the spoon's bowl. All of very similar dimensions, they can be described as 'standard issue' and identified as German Second World War army *Göffeln* – a portmanteau word equivalent to 'spork', from *Gabel* (fork) joined with *Löffel* (spoon). Within the group, some bear official inspection proof marks, and others manufacturers' marks indicating production in 1938 or 1940. Some also have engraved initials, or names – including 'R Wagner', who owned this example.

These German army sporks are not the only Second World War finds reported from the area. Two buttons have been found, one a British Army General Service example and the other of the *Kreigsmarine* (navy) of Nazi Germany. These, with other finds, suggest a prisoner-of-war (POW) camp – one which included captured U-boat crews. This camp was possibly located by geophysical survey during work at the famous early medieval site of Cottam B. On 11 September 1945, POW Camp 163 moved from Butterwick, to the north, to 'Langtoft near Driffield', but the exact location wasn't given in the records. This military material, with the previous geophysics, provides strong evidence for the location of the new camp, or part of it, to the west of Langtoft.

German Second World War army spork (YORYM-1834FA).

Other material evidence for POW camps includes this plaque from Utkinton, Cheshire, 68 mm long (LVPL-4C8B6D). It apparently bears an individual's POW number and place of capture.

Work, Money and Trade

While for someone from 1500 most of our world would be very strange, one of the few things that would seem instantly familiar would be coinage. Coins are still round discs of metal with the king's head on one side. The extensive use of credit would also be familiar, although today's regulated banks and state-issued paper money are very different.

In contrast, the type of work people do, how they do it, and where, changed completely over the period covered in this book. In 1500 about three-quarters of England's population's main occupation was agriculture. About a fifth of jobs were in manufacturing, mostly producing cloth, clothing and shoes, and less than 10 per cent were in services, from teaching and medicine to retail. Now less than 1 per cent of the population works in agriculture, 80 per cent in services. Post-medieval people produced many more of the goods and food they needed within their own household. The household unit was very different, however, often including servants and apprentices.

Education in a formal setting was experienced only by the tiniest minority in 1500. By 1600 more people got at least some formal schooling and by 1700 over 50 per cent of people could read, at least a little.

The merchant and his wife by Marinus van Reymerswaele (1540). Their triangular heads deliberately echo the triangular pans of the coin weighing scale. Note also the special box for a set of various coin weights. (Courtesy of the Statens Museum for Kunst, Copenhagen/Europeana)

42. Gold half sovereign of Henry VIII (NCL-B02245)
1544–47
Found on Lindisfarne, Northumberland, in 2011. Weight 6.25 g.

Medieval English coins show an idealised king, regardless of what the ruler looked like – often the design didn't even change between reigns. Starting with Henry VII in 1504, rulers chose to be shown as recognisable individuals, usually in profile as on modern coins, although the portraits are, of course, still flattering. The gold coin called the 'sovereign' was originally introduced in 1489 and was worth one pound and one shilling, or 252 pennies. It was normally used for large payments and royal gifts. It would take a foot soldier forty-two days to earn one and it could buy two cows or pay around six months' rent on a one-room cottage. A new sovereign coin, worth one pound (20 shillings), was introduced in 1817 and continues to be made for special presentations and collectors today.

This coin was found as part of a group hidden in a jug which had been buried near a house on the island of Lindisfarne. It was discovered when digging out an old water pipe and is thought to have been buried in the early 1560s. This might have been in response to the Civil War in nearby Scotland, or the owner may have been saving up for a future purchase and had personal reasons to be worried about their coins' safety.

Above: Front of the gold half sovereign (NCL-B02245).

Right: The jug with the group of coins found in it.

In 2016, a hoard of 633 gold sovereigns and 280 half sovereigns was found inside an old piano in Bishop's Castle, Shropshire (HESH-F5F412). The coins, dating from 1847 to 1915, were found stitched into cloth packages and a purse and hidden under the keyboard. The piano had been donated to a community college and, when no owner or claimants could be found, the money went to the school.

43. Hoard of silver coin clippings (GLO-0794E0)
1662–90
Found in Littledean, Gloucestershire, in 2015. Weight 323 g.

Coin clipping – cutting slivers of precious metal from the edge of a coin – was a common crime in the sixteenth and seventeenth centuries. Unlike modern coins, hand-struck coins were already slightly irregular in shape, so cuts were less obvious. To stop clipping words or patterns were put on the coin's sides; machines to do this were developed in the 1660s and we continue to do it today. Clippings would be melted down and often used to make counterfeit coins, the silver mixed with cheaper copper and lead. People would regularly weigh the coins offered to them, to check they hadn't been clipped, as in the painting at the start of this chapter. Coin weights for gold coins are more common finds than the precious metal coins themselves.

Clipping and counterfeiting were countered with tough laws and extreme punishment, often execution. Clippings would have been melted down as quickly as possible to destroy any evidence, so it is rare to find them. This hoard is the biggest group ever found in England. The latest identified fragment dates to 1662, so they may be from the monetary crisis of the 1680s and 1690s. At that point the coins in use were often 100 or 150 years old and had become very worn and clipped. The more people got used to clipped coins, the more criminals could get away with clipping them. People hoarded the better coins and refused to spend them. In the end the government had to call in all the coins and remake them, just as they recently did with British pound coins. This 'Great Recoinage' of 1697 was managed by Sir Isaac Newton, famous for describing the mathematics of gravity.

Hoard of coin clippings (GLO-0794E0).

The arms and initials on this coin weight show it was made in Middelburg in the Netherlands by Isaac Gz Deelen I, between 1585 and 1620. The facing busts are Ferdinand and Isabella of Spain (1469–1504), indicating the weight was for an *excellente*, a coin issued across their European lands. Found in Charleton, Devon, with two others from the same set, 15 mm in width (DEV-C06118).

44. Copper-alloy token halfpenny of Eleazar Hugman (LON-F69276)
1666
Found on the Thames foreshore in London, in 2012. Diameter 21 mm.

As well as state-issued coins, the PAS records a wide range of what are called 'paranumismatica', ranging from Elizabethan lead tokens to nineteenth-century tool checks. These were often used locally and unofficially and therefore can be hard to relate to a particular person or use. Seventeenth-century trade tokens like this were designed to circulate alongside state coinage, supplementing supply when the state wasn't issuing enough coins, or those coins weren't reaching the areas they needed to. Because they were supposed to circulate to more people, they usually have the name of the issuer and their place of business, so people knew where to go to trade them back for goods or official coinage. They also provided an excellent way to advertise people's businesses.

In 1666 Eleazar Hugman lived in Southwark, next to the Bridge House, which held the material for repairing the old London Bridge – a huge structure which was covered along its length with houses and grand buildings. We know his name, where he lived and a bit about his job because he issued this token. Distilling had been used for centuries to make perfumes and medicines. In the seventeenth century new designs of stills, and cheaper copper imports, made them more affordable. The large jug into which the liquid is being distilled is a type normally used for serving drinks, suggesting Hugman was distilling a spirit like gin, vodka or even rum from new sugar imports.

Eleazar Hugman's token (LON-F69276).

A token issued in 1664 in 'Sunning Town', probably Sonning in Berkshire, which shows a large sugar cone, found on the Thames foreshore in London, 16 mm in diameter (ESS-162FED). Sugar was becoming more available in England in this period with the expansion of cultivation in the Caribbean, increasingly supported by a horrific slave trade.

Idealised view of enslaved people bringing sugar cane to be crushed so the juice could be extracted. William Clark, the artist, was invited to Antigua in 1832 by plantation owners, perhaps to counter anti-slavery campaigns in England; his images show nothing of the hardship or violence of slavery. (Courtesy of the British Library, London/Unsplash)

45. Copper-alloy coin hoard (HAMP-E4E185)
c. 1711
Found in Bishops Waltham, Hampshire, in 2010. Weight *c.* 26 kg overall.

Foreign trade and connections can be studied through the distribution of coins that have arrived from overseas. However, the presence of this group of French coins, found under the floorboards of a Hampshire shop during repairs to the plumbing, may not be so straightforward. Comprising 7,083 coins, this cache appears to consist entirely of the same type of coin – the 30-denier piece. Intriguingly, despite the thousands found under this shop floor, no other examples have been found in England.

The 30-denier piece was known as a 'mousquetaire' (musketeer), as the cross on the reverse resembles the emblem of the French king's guard. It was a short-lived type, only made for five years, struck in France specifically for use in Canada and Louisiana. Where readable, the coins found in Bishops Waltham could all be identified as being struck in Lyon in 1711, during the reign of Louis XIV.

But evidently this was not simply a batch intercepted on its journey from France. Close examination revealed that the coins displayed various inconsistencies, such as discrepancies in size or silver coating. This led to the conclusion that they were all forgeries made from the same die, maybe a stolen official one. Perhaps they represent an English attempt to flood the French colonies with fake coins – if so, the attempt ended in failure.

Hoard of 7,083 French colonial coins from the early eighteenth century (HAMP-E4E185). But are they genuine issues?

Detail of one of the 30-denier pieces from the hoard.

This rare silver 'Oak tree' threepence was issued by the colony of Massachusetts, North America, in the 1660s. Piercing of coins, perhaps for wearing or sewing them to clothes to keep them safe, was common in this period. Pierced or foreign coins could still pass as currency by weight, or for their nominal value. Found near Ebchester, County Durham, 16 mm in diameter (NCL-7C60CD).

46. Silver and steel thimble (NARC-7C4411)
1771–90
Found in Preston Capes, Northamptonshire, in 2011. Height 21 mm.

Silver thimbles were an affordable bit of luxury in the seventeenth and eighteenth centuries. This one is made of separate sides and top, with machine stamped and rolled decoration on the sides, making it quicker, and thus cheaper, to produce. The thimble had a steel cap to protect the top, improving its functionality and using less silver.

The maker's mark shows it was made in the workshop of Hester Bateman, a noted London silversmith in the late eighteenth century. She is famed for her spoons, and other domestic goods such as teapots, but finds recorded by the PAS show her workshop made a full range of small goods including thimbles, small seal matrices and buckles.

Hester was born in London around 1708 and married a wire drawer and gold chain maker. When her husband died in 1760 he left her his tools, indicating that he already expected her to take over the workshop. She was very successful, building up the firm to a large business specialising in elegant but popular pieces at competitive prices. She invested in new technology and used standardised and repeated designs to drive up production and reduce costs. By 1786 she employed forty silversmiths in her workshop. Retiring in 1790, she passed the business on to her sons, Jonathan and Peter. After Jonathan's death Peter went into business with his sister-in-law, Ann, continuing the female management.

Thimble with 'H B' maker's mark
(NARC-7C4411).

47. Lead cloth seal (HAMP-C2E516)
1660–85
Found in Ringwood, Hampshire, in 2012. Length 28 mm.

The cloth trade was one of England's most important export industries from at least the twelfth century and up until the twentieth century. Originally the focus was on exporting wool, but during the fifteenth and sixteenth centuries domestic weaving industries became increasingly important. Merchant clothiers often managed their workers through 'putting out' systems where they provided the raw materials and paid for the finished thread, or cloth. Skilled spinners (mostly women) and weavers (mostly men) and their families, who sometimes helped, worked at home and had some flexibility to fit this work around other tasks such as growing food, keeping animals, or childcare.

Certain areas became well known for the quality or style of their woollen cloth, in particular the West Country broad cloths and the East Anglian Bays and Says. This latter industry was encouraged by the arrival of skilled clothworkers from the Continent, like Protestant Huguenots from France, refugees because of their religious beliefs. The cloth seldom survives but lead seals were used to track all parts of the process, for quality control, proof of origin and proof of tax and export checks. These seals were attached to the edge of the cloth and discarded when it was used. They are found across England and abroad. The legend on this example shows this was an alnage (tax) seal and that the cloth was made in Yorkshire, although it was found in Hampshire where the cloth was used. The 'K' probably stands for Kersey, a cheap woollen cloth.

Seventeenth-century cloth seal for Yorkshire cloth (HAMP-C2E516).

Above: The other disc from this seal has broken away showing the impression of the striped cloth to which it was attached. The seal comes from Turnhout in modern-day Belgium, which in the sixteenth century was noted for producing 'ticking' for making bedlinen. Found in Wonston, Hampshire, 28 mm in width (HAMP-19B0F2).

Right: This seal is a personal, rather than official one. The elaborate merchant's mark, which combines symbols and the initials I(M)P, would have identified the weaver, searcher or dyer to others who traded with them. Found in Llangain, Carmarthenshire, 21 mm in width (NMGW-039649).

Searchers examining a cloth for faults as one applies a lead seal to the edge of the cloth. (Detail from a painting by Isaac van Swanenburg, 1594–96, courtesy of the Museum de Lakenhal, Leiden)

48. Folded silver sixpence of George II (ESS-E5C826)
1727–60
Found in Little Maplestead, Essex, in 2011. Diameter 21 mm.

As small, sometimes inexpensive, pieces of decorative metal, coins were often reused for other purposes. Drilling a few holes could convert them into a button or pendant, or more elaborate reshaping could turn them into a ring or toy, like the 'Penny spitfire' in the introduction. In the late seventeenth and eighteenth century coins were turned into charms and into tokens to be exchanged by lovers. These coins could be rubbed smooth on one face and engraved with names and messages. Other coins were simply folded twice into an S-shape to make a 'love' token. Used as good luck charms as well as exchanged between lovers, these are the original 'crooked sixpence' of the nursery rhyme.

Worn and folded silver sixpence of George II (ESS-E5C826).

Some modifications weren't designed to remove coins from circulation. Small value coins change hands frequently, they are therefore an excellent way to spread a message, either the official message the coin makers, and ruler, wanted to send, or in this case a public appeal for change. The WSPU refers to the Women's Social and Political Union, founded in 1903. The WSPU promoted direct action to achieve the vote, including criminal damage and hunger strikes. Defacing a coin in this way was illegal but spread the message every time it changed hands.

Counterstamped 1899 penny of Victoria. Found on the Thames foreshore in London, 26 mm in diameter (LON-ED928E).

A counterstamped 'spade guinea'. These were fake coins produced as gaming chips. The counter stamping, and findspot, suggests this was a colliery check, used to keep track of how many miners were underground, or the tools and lamps they signed out. Found in Treorchy, Rhondda Cynon Taf, 25 mm in diameter (GGAT-FEC976).

49. Copper-alloy 'manilla' (GAT-649317)
1550–1945
Found in Llandwrog, Gwynedd, in 1995. Length 61 mm.

This penannular copper-alloy ring with flared terminals was produced in Britain for trade with West African countries. Manillas were mass produced in standardised sizes to act as currency items, and stayed very similar in form for several centuries. They were designed to mimic the bracelets and leg bands used in West Africa to store and display wealth prior to extensive sea-trade with Europe. When they reached the African coast they might be traded further inland or melted down for recasting into locally made and desired objects, such as the Benin Bronzes.

Manillas were used in large numbers as part of the 'triangular' trade when European ships carried trade goods to Africa to purchase local goods and people. These enslaved people were transported in terrible conditions to the Americas, mostly to work making sugar, tobacco and, later, cotton, which would be shipped back to meet consumer demand in Europe.

Manilla (GAT-649317).

50. Fused lumps of mixed metal (PUBLIC-8ECB27)
2008
Found in Weston-super-Mare, North Somerset, in 2017. Length of largest piece: 120 mm.

In 2008 the end of Weston's Grand Pier, and its pavilion, burned to the waterline. Up to £100,000 in cash was thought to have been melted and mangled in the fire, mostly from the pier's 370 slot machines. These three melted, fused lumps of metal are still in some places recognisable as coins: a mix of 50, 20, 10 and 5ps.

The pieces were found in the shingle near the new pavilion. These physical remains are modern but could provide archaeologists of the future with a snapshot of the low-value coinage in use at the time. In their fused and twisted state, they also provide a tangible sense of the heat of the fire, a link to a dramatic, disastrous, moment which was important for the town. While the loss of the pier seemed to symbolise the decline of this seaside resort, the decision to rebuild it was welcomed as evidence of hope for the town's regeneration.

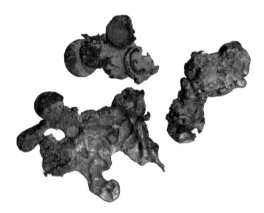

Left: Three groups of melted coins from the 2008 fire that destroyed Weston's Grand Pier (PUBLIC-8ECB27).

Below: The rebuilt Weston Pier. Seaside holidays first became popular in the eighteenth century in Britain but many resorts declined with the advent of cheap foreign flights in the late twentieth. (Image by Ollie Taylor/Shutterstock.com)

Useful Resources

All the finds in this book are recorded on the Portable Antiquities Scheme database and you can read much more about them there: finds.org.uk/database. The Scheme's website also provides very useful guides to different types of finds.

If you are interested in learning more about specific archaeological sites across England and Wales then data from most local Historic Environment Records have been brought together at heritagegateway.org.uk

The Society for Post-Medieval Archaeology (SPMA) and Finds Research Group (for finds from AD 700–1700) publish academic work on finds from this period. Every year a round-up of important finds recorded by the PAS appears in the SPMA journal – many round-ups can also be accessed on the PAS website. There are also many special interest societies focussed on particular types of objects, from buttons and coins to pewter and pottery.

Locally, there are many active history and archaeology societies who run talks, events and even excavations. Nationally, the Society of Antiquaries of London makes many of their lectures available free online, as does the Institute for Historical Research.

This book relies on many previous publications; it is not possible to list them all here but we acknowledge again our debt to previous scholars and find recorders.

Silver toothpick and nail cleaning kit of 1600–50 that previously fitted into the handle of a folding spoon and fork set. Most people carried a simple eating knife with them, picking up food with the point. Forks were introduced in the seventeenth century and it gradually became expected a host would supply cutlery for visitors. Found in Mareham Le Fen, Lincolnshire, 105 mm high (LIN-4D7C18).

Information about the PAS

The PAS records archaeological finds made by members of the public through their network of Finds Liaison Officers (FLOs). They are always keen to hear about your finds and make detailed records of as many as they can. Contact details for all the local FLOs can be found on the PAS website: finds.org.uk.

The Scheme covers England and Wales; Scotland, Northern Ireland and the Isles have different systems and laws about finds and metal detecting. FLOs also deal with Treasure; not always as exciting as it sounds, this is legally defined material which is considered property of the Crown and must be reported to the coroner. More details of the Treasure Act, what constitutes Treasure, and how to report it can be found from your local FLO or at finds.org.uk/treasure.

If you are planning to look for objects, by fieldwalking or metal detecting you must have permission of the landowner. All land, even verges and beaches, has a landowner. Apart from Treasure, all finds belong to the landowner so you must agree with them in advance what will happen to anything you find.

Please do report your finds so they can continue to add to everyone's knowledge. Every small piece of pottery or worn coin is an important part of building a larger picture and learning more about the past of your area.

Laura Burnett discussing finds with their finder.